My Train Set

By Annette Smith

Photographs by Lyz Turner-Clark

This is my train set.

My train set is in a big box.

The train has an engine and three carriages.

The engine is red.
The carriages are blue.

My train set has
lots of tracks.

The train goes
on the tracks.

The train can go

over the big bridge.

The train can go into the little tunnel.

My train set has a station.

A man looks after the station.

I like my train set.